D1372901

DECLARATION

•

I hereby declare that
all the paper produced
by Cartiere del Garda S.p.A.
in its Riva del Garda mill
is manufactured completely
Acid-free and Wood-free

Dr. Alois Lueftinger
Managing Director and General Manager
Cartiere del Garda S.p.A.

GREEN WORLD

TREES OF THE TROPICS

Written by
Jennifer Cochrane

STECK-VAUGHN
LIBRARY
A Division of Steck-Vaughn Company

Austin, Texas

**Published in the United States in 1991
by Steck-Vaughn, Co., Austin, Texas,**
a subsidiary of National Education Corporation

A Templar Book
Devised and produced by The Templar Company plc
Pippbrook Mill, London Road, Dorking, Surrey RH4 1JE, Great Britain
Copyright © 1990 by The Templar Company plc

Editor: Wendy Madgwick
Designer: Jane Hunt
Illustrator: Sallie Reason

Notes to Reader
There are some words in this book that are printed in **bold** type.
A brief explanation of these words is given in the glossary on p. 44.

All living things are given two Latin names when first classified
by a scientist. Some of them also have a common name, for example the
papaya, *Carica papaya*. In this book, the common name is used where
possible, but the scientific name is given when first mentioned.

Library of Congress Cataloging-in-Publication Data
Cochrane, Jennifer.
Trees of the tropics / written by Jennifer Cochrane.
p. cm. – (The Green World)
"A Templar Book" – T.p. verso.
Includes bibliographical references and index.
Summary: Discusses tropical forests and trees of various areas of the world.
ISBN 0-8114-2731-5
1. Trees – Tropics – Juvenile literature.   2. Tropical plants – Juvenile
literature.   3. Rain forests–Juvenile literature.
[1. Trees – Tropics.   2. Tropical plants.   3. Rain forests.]
I. Title.   II. Series.
QK474.5.C63   1991   90-10023
582.160909'3–dc20   CIP AC

Color separations by Positive Colour Ltd, Maldon, Essex, Great Britain
Printed and bound by L.E.G.O., Vicenza, Italy
1 2 3 4 5 6 7 8 9 0   LE 95 94 93 92 91

Photographic credits
t = top, b = bottom, l = left, r = right
Cover: Bruce Coleman; page 10 Frank Lane/Silvestris; page 11
Frank Lane/L. Norstrom; page 13 Bruce Coleman/Peter Wood; page 14
Bruce Coleman/G. Ziesler; page 17 Bruce Coleman/N. Devore; page 18
Frank Lane/S.C. Bisserot; page 20 Bruce Coleman/Eric Crichton;
page 25 Frank Lane/Silvestris; page 29 Bruce Coleman/L.C. Marigo; page
31*t* Frank Lane/Permaphotos Wildlife; page 31*b* Bruce Coleman/
P. Davey; page 36 Frank Lane/Holt Studios; page 37*t* Frank Lane/
Holt Studios; page 37*b* Frank Lane/Holt Studios; page 38 Greenpeace;
page 39 Frank Lane/Holt Studios; page 41 Bruce Coleman/N.G. Blake;
page 42 Frank Lane/A. Parker; page 43*t* WWF/Mauri Rautkari; page 43*b*
Hollandse Hoogte/H. Wallrafen.

CONTENTS

GREEN WORLD

This tree shows the different groups of plants that are found in the world. It does not show how they developed or their relationship with each other.

There are thousands of tropical trees, but they can be grouped according to their uses.

Group 1
- Trees that give food – coconuts, bananas, dates

Group 2
- Trees that give fuel – oil palm, babassu palm

MONOCOTYLEDONS

DICOTYLEDONS

CONIFEROUS (OR FIR) TREES (Gymnosperms)

FLOWERING PLANTS (Angiosperms)

Group 1
- Trees that give food – cocoa, mango, brazil nuts

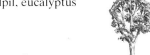

Group 2
- Trees that give fuel – ipilpil, eucalyptus

Group 1
- Trees that give food – sago palm

Group 3
- Trees that give timber – mahogany, ebony, teak

FERNS, CLUBMOSSES, AND HORSETAILS (Pteridophytes)

Group 4
- Trees that give medicines – quinine, coca

MOSSES AND LIVERWORTS (Bryophytes)

ALGAE

GREEN PLANTS

Group 5
- Trees that give spices – clove, nutmeg

ANIMALS

PLANTS

FUNGI AND LICHENS

BACTERIA

SLIME MOLD

LIVING THINGS

Group 6
- Trees that give shade – acacia, eucalyptus, baobab

6

The land area of the world is divided into ten large zones depending on the plants that grow there. Tropical trees grow in the area between the Tropics of Cancer and Capricorn.

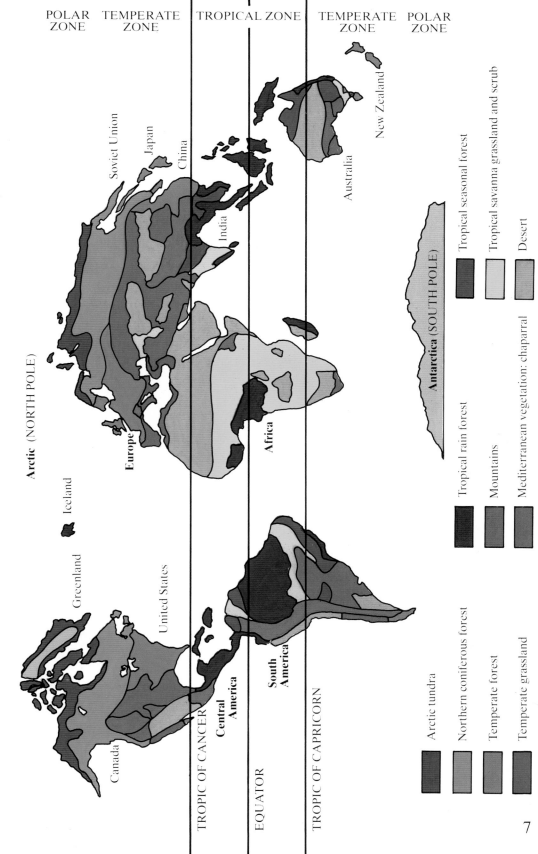

POLAR ZONE   TEMPERATE ZONE   TROPICAL ZONE   TEMPERATE ZONE   POLAR ZONE

TROPIC OF CANCER

EQUATOR

TROPIC OF CAPRICORN

Arctic (NORTH POLE)

Soviet Union
Japan
China
India
Europe
Africa
Iceland
Greenland
United States
Canada
Central America
South America
Australia
New Zealand
Antarctica (SOUTH POLE)

Arctic tundra
Northern coniferous forest
Temperate forest
Temperate grassland

Tropical rain forest
Mountains
Mediterranean vegetation: chaparral

Tropical seasonal forest
Tropical savanna grassland and scrub
Desert

TROPICAL TREES

It is not easy to describe a tropical tree, because there are so many different kinds. A few belong to the cone-bearers, the **gymnosperms**, but most are flower-bearers, the **angiosperms**. There are thousands of kinds, including straight-leaved palm trees, fruit trees, timber trees, and spice trees. Tropical trees also grow in many different **habitats**, including swamps, mountains, islands, forests, and deserts.

The link between all these different trees is the area in which they grow – the tropics. The tropics is the area between the Tropic of Cancer in the north and the Tropic of Capricorn in the south. The equator runs through the middle of it. This is the part of the planet where the sun is straight overhead at noon. It is the sunniest, hottest part of the world.

It is the hot, bright sunlight that helps so many different trees to grow in the tropics. Trees, like all green plants, make their own food from carbon dioxide gas in the air and water and minerals from the soil. With sunlight, the trees combine these chemicals to make sugar, which is then made into starches, proteins, and fats (see p. 22).

The date palm (*Phoenix dactylifera*) is found in tropical and subtropical areas.

The cycad (*Cycas revoluta*; a gymnosperm) is a "living fossil" from Australia and New Guinea.

Diptocarpus species are found in tropical Asia.

Sunny and hot

There are two reasons for the greater amount of sunlight in the tropics. The first is the shape of the planet. If a circular beam of sunlight shone on the equator, it would light a circle the same width across as the beam. If the same size beam shone on the polar regions, it would light up a much larger area. The sunlight would be spread out. The reason for this is the way the spherical planet slopes away from the sun at the poles.

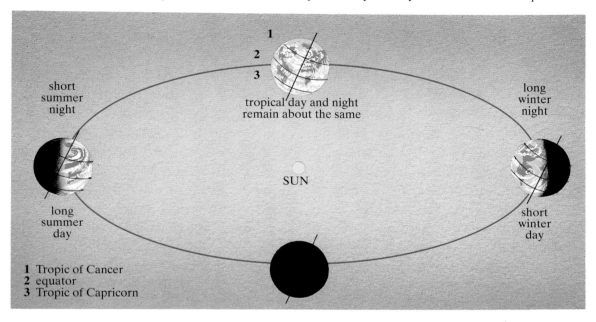

short summer night

long summer day

tropical day and night remain about the same

SUN

long winter night

short winter day

1 Tropic of Cancer
2 equator
3 Tropic of Capricorn

Balsa trees (*Ochroma lagopus*) provide the lightest-known timber.

The second reason is the tilt of the Earth on its axis as it travels around the sun in a year. The angle at which the Earth is tilted means that the lands nearer the poles have long days in the summer and short nights. In the winter they have short days and long nights, and they are colder. However, in the tropics there is not much difference in the length of the days and nights during the year and the temperature is about the same throughout the year.

■ Tropical trees are found between the Tropics of Cancer and Capricorn.
■ Both gymnosperms and angiosperms are found in the tropics.
■ Most tropical trees are found in the tropical rain forests.
■ More species of trees are found in tropical forests than anywhere else in the world.
■ Many tropical trees are cultivated by people for their fruits, nuts, and spices, as well as for their timber.

WHERE THEY GROW

Tropical trees, like all the other plants on Earth, grow together in large groups called **biomes**. The kind of biome in the tropics is decided by the amount of rain that falls. There are six large biomes in the tropics – tropical rain forest, tropical seasonal forest, tropical grassland, mountain, semidesert, and desert. There are also some small biomes such as swamps and islands.

The plants that grow in a biome affect the soil on which they grow. Poor soil can be made more fertile when rotting leaves and dead plants are mixed into it. Tropical soil is usually poor since the leaves rot away very quickly, before they can be mixed into the soil. Also, heavy rains **leach** or wash the mineral salts such as nitrates and phosphates down into the soil, out of reach of the plants growing on the surface. In dry places, few plants can grow and so few leaves are shed to be mixed into the soil to help hold the rainwater.

Forests that have not been changed are called primary forests. Those that have been cut or burned down and have grown again are called secondary forests.

Rain forests

True rain forest has over 155 inches of rain falling on it in a year. The evergreen moist rain forest has between 75 and 155 inches of rainfall. The rain falls all through the year in these forests, and tropical rain forests have no seasons. Rain forests are found in Central America, in the north of South America, in West Africa, west India, Southeast Asia, and Indonesia.

Mountains may receive plenty of water, but they are cold at the top, and trees do not grow there. Lower down the slopes coniferous trees grow, and lower still, seasonal forests grow. Tropical rain forests can grow up to 5,900 feet in the Amazon and up to 2,500 feet in Southeast Asia.

Seasonal forests

Tropical seasonal forests do have seasons. They have a dry season, when no rain falls, and a wet season with between 20 and 75 inches of rainfall. Seasonal forests are called monsoon forests in some places. In the dry season, the leaves turn brown and fall, and the sun can reach the plants on the ground. There are more ground plants in seasonal forests than in true rain forests. Seasonal forests are found in Australia, India, Indonesia, Africa, and Central and South America.

Tropical grasslands

Tropical grasslands have a yearly rainfall of 8 to 20 inches. The trees are spaced out so that they can collect water from a wide area. The African baobab stores water in its spongy trunk.

African baobab
(*Adansonia digitata*)

Semideserts

Semideserts only have 4 to 8 inches of rain in a year. A few scrubby trees can survive on that small amount of water. Trees only grow around oases in desert regions.

CENTRAL & SOUTH AMERICA

The tropical forests of Central and South America cover about 2 million square miles. They include the largest primary forests in the world. No one knows just how many different trees grow there, possibly thousands.

In the Choco region of Colombia, **botanists** (people who study plants) found 208 different kinds of trees in just a quarter acre. The same area farther north would contain about 18 species. The forests of the Americas probably have a million different plants and animals living in them.

There are five biomes in the region. The Sierra Madre mountains in Central America and the Andes on the west side of South America have a dry semidesert strip between them and the Pacific Ocean. The Amazon rain forest surrounds the Amazon River and stretches from the Andes eastward to the Atlantic Ocean. There are patches of seasonal forest in eastern Brazil and Venezuela and tropical grassland, or pampas, in southern Brazil.

Mahogany Tree
(*Swietenia mahogani*)
This tree grows on the Caribbean island of Hispaniola. Mahogany is still used to make furniture, but all 23 kinds of mahogany are endangered.

Rubber Tree
(*Hevea braziliensis*)
This tree originally grew under taller trees in Amazonia. It is now cultivated on rubber plantations throughout Indonesia.

Coconut Palm
(*Cocos nucifera*)
This is often the only tree on small desert islands. The light, buoyant coconut fruit floats easily, carrying the seed across the bodies of water.

Useful trees

Many useful trees are found in this region. There are many timber trees, including rosewood (*Dalbergia* species), greenheart (*Nectandra roediei*), and balsa. Guavas (*Pisidium guajava*) and avocado pears (*Persea americana*) have been taken from the forest and grown on plantations for their fruits. The coca shrub (*Erythroxylon coca*) from the Andes gives the drug cocaine. Allspice (*Pimenta dioica*) adds flavor to foods. The ipilpil (*Leucana leucocephala*) provides both fuel and animal feed. There may be many more useful trees in the unexplored parts of the rain forests.

Cocoa Tree (*Theobroma cacao*)
This small tree grows in Amazonia. Chocolate is made from its seeds. The trees were taken to Africa and Indonesia in the 1600s and still grow there on plantations.

Brazil Nut Tree (*Bertholletia excelsa*)
This is a tall tree growing in Amazonia. The nuts or seeds, which are edible, are contained in woody pods.

Cinchona (*Cinchona ledgeriana*)
This tree grows in the Andes and was taken to Europe in the 1600s. The medicine quinine, which is used to treat malaria, is made from its bark.

13

TREES OF AFRICA

Africa is drier than Asia and South America. There is the Sahara Desert in the north of the African tropics, and semidesert and grassland, called savanna, in the east and south. Africa has the smallest area of primary tropical rain forest. There are 700,000 square miles, with 500,000 square miles of it growing around the Congo, or Zaire, river system. The rest of the rain forest is along the south coast of West Africa, around the mouths of the Niger and Volta rivers. There is mountain forest on the Ethiopian highlands and the Mitumba mountains. The Congo River rises in the Mitumba mountains and flows west for 1,688 miles to the Atlantic Ocean.

Africa's forests do not have as many kinds of trees on one acre of land as American and Asian forests. There are probably about 330,000 different plants and animals in African tropical forests. The island of Madagascar, on the east coast, is the richest area for wildlife in Africa. Its rain forest is about 9,250 square miles in area and about 12,000 different kinds of plants grow there. For example, there are nine **species** of baobab trees growing in Madagascar and only one in the rest of Africa.

African rain forests

The dense African rain forest has many useful trees in it. Many of these are timber trees. Obeche (*Triplochiton scleroxylon*) and afrormosia (*Pericopsis elata*) are used in building and furniture-making. Ebony (*Diospyros mespiliformis*) also grows there; its wood is used to make piano keys. The forest plants provide many drugs and medicines, which help to cure asthma and eye diseases, among others. Melegueta pepper (*Aframomum melegueta*) is collected to use as a spice. In the dry areas, the baobab supplies fiber to make ropes and nets.

Date Palm
(*Phoenix dactylifera*)
This palm grows near water in the desert. People have taken date palms and planted them all over the tropics, but scientists think that they first grew in Arabia and North Africa.

Doum Palm
(*Hyphaene theobaica*)
This palm grows in the semidesert, in the Sudan. The fruits are eaten, and the hard, white seeds, which are often called vegetable ivory, can be carved into ornaments.

African Oil Palm
(*Elaeis guineensis*)
This palm grows in the rain forests. The oil palm is also grown on plantations for its oil. The oil from the seeds is used to make margarine and soap. Oil is also made from the fruit.

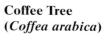

Thorn or Gum Arabic Tree
(*Acacia senegal*)
Thorn trees grow in forests in dry areas, and in grasslands. The thorns do not stop giraffes from eating thorn trees. These trees improve the soil and give gum arabic, used in cooking and to make sweets.

Sapele
(*Entandophragma cylindricum*)
This tree grows in the West African rain forest. It is one of the giants, growing up to 150 feet high, and reaching 20 feet around the trunk. The wood is called African mahogany.

Coffee Tree
(*Coffea arabica*)
This tree grows wild in the Ethiopian highlands. The Arabs discovered in the 1500s that the roasted beans made a delicious hot drink. It is now grown on plantations in India, Indonesia, Brazil, and the West Indies.

TREES OF ASIA

The tropical forests of Asia cover 800,000 square miles, many of them on islands. These island forests have given rise to about 750,000 different plants and animals. There are over 20,000 islands along the coasts of Asia, stretching across the sea toward Australia. Forests are found in India, Burma, Thailand, Vietnam and Cambodia, and south in Malaysia and Indonesia. Many of their coasts are protected by mangrove swamps.

Each island has its own plants and animals, although some species are found on all of them. Malaysia alone has 2,500 different trees. Some grow nowhere else. Asian tropical forests have about 40 kinds of tree on one acre in the dry areas, and 80 in the wet lowlands.

Many of the fruits eaten today began life in the Asian tropical forests. More than half the **hardwood** timber comes from the forests of tropical Asia. Teak (*Tectona grandis*), tropical oaks (*Castanopsis* species), and walnuts (*Dracontomelum* species) are used for shipbuilding, house building, and to make furniture.

Banyan
(*Ficus bengalensis*)
If a banyan seed drops on the branch of another tree, it sends down roots and side branches. The banyan is a network of branches, trunks, and roots.

Teak
(*Tectona grandis*)
This tree grows up to 150 feet high and can measure 40 feet around its trunk. Its leaves are high in the forest canopy. It is a valuable timber tree.

Mangroves
(*Rhizophora* species)
Mangroves grow on coasts and in estuaries in all tropical forests. The mass of mangrove roots keep the soil from washing away.

Mango
(*Mangifera indica*)
Mangos are grown in India, Burma, and Malaysia on plantations. Its fruits are eaten fresh, or made into chutney.

Nutmeg
(*Myrica fragrans*)
This tree grows in Indonesia. The seeds are used to make the spice nutmeg and the fruit is dried to make the spice mace.

Sago Palm
(*Metroxylon sago*)
This tree grows in the swamps of Southeast Asia. The food sago is made from the pith inside the trunk.

Spice Islands
The Spice Islands were given their name because so many species were found there. Nutmeg, cinnamon (*Cinnamomum zeylanicum*), and cloves (*Eugenia caryophyllata*) were all found in the Moluccas, and ginger (*Zingiber officinale*), cardomom (*Elletaria cardamomum*), and pepper (*Piper nigrum*) grow wild in Asia.

TROPICAL AUSTRALIA

The trees of Australia and New Guinea are not like the trees in the rest of the world. The reason for this is that the Australian continent separated from the rest of the land on Earth about 135 million years ago. All the living things in that area have slowly changed over millions of years to give plants and animals that are unlike those found on other continents.

The biomes are the same as those in the rest of the tropics. There are tropical rain forests, monsoon forests, and mountain forests in New Guinea and northern Australia. There is no great river system in Australia, and the wettest parts of the land are those near the coast. Mangrove swamps edge the north coast of Australia and the coast of New Guinea. The Australian forests are monsoon forests, which have a dry season, and away from the sea it is very dry. Therefore, unlike rain forests, only a few kinds of tree grow there and they do not grow close together.

Many useful and unusual trees grow in Australia. Timber, mostly southern beech (*Nothofagus* species) and oak, is exported in large quantities from New Guinea. Bunya pines (*Araucaria bidwilli*) are gymnosperms, related to fir trees. The seeds in their cones are collected and eaten by aborigines.

Ancient trees
The cycads were important trees 270 million years ago. *Cycas media* can be found in the rain forests of New Guinea and Australia. Cycads can live for hundreds of years.

**Screw Pine
(*Pandanus odoratissimus*)**
This tree grows in marshes in
New Guinea and north
Australia. It is named after the
pattern that the seeds make on
the pineapple-like fruit. Stilt
roots support it in the mud.

**Grass Tree
(*Kingsia australis*)**
The leaves of the grass tree
look like grass. As the leaves
grow and die, new leaves
appear higher up the tree. The
leaf bases left behind can be
used to determine its age.

**Sydney Blue Gum Tree
(*Eucalyptus saligna*)**
There are 400 different kinds
of gum tree in Australia and
New Guinea. Gum trees have
evolved only in Australia.
They are very adaptable and
are now planted worldwide.

**She-oak
(*Casuarina equisitifolia*)**
This tree grows beside streams,
on beaches, and in monsoon
forests in Australia and New
Guinea. It can survive long dry
periods. It has tough timber.

**Moreton Bay Chestnut
(*Castanospernum australe*)**
This tree is not a chestnut, but
it has seeds that are good to
eat. The timber is called black
bean because of the black
pattern in it.

**Honeysuckle Tree
(*Banksia marginata*)**
The banksias, or honeysuckle
trees, attract many bees to
their colorful, nectar-laden
flowers, which are arranged in
upright spires.

TRUNKS AND ROOTS

Trees all have the same basic pattern: branching roots, strong stems, which may branch, and a **crown** of broad leaves or pine needles. The roots anchor the plant in the ground, and take in water and mineral salts from the soil. In tropical rain forests there is plenty of water, so roots do not have to grow deep to reach it. However, mineral salts are in short supply (see p. 10) so the plants survive by reusing minerals. When the leaves, twigs, and dead plants fall to the ground, the process of decay begins. Many tropical trees have a wide circle of shallow roots which may stick up above the ground. These surface roots take in the salts that dissolve from the plant debris as it decays before they can be washed away by the heavy rainfall.

The stem takes water from the roots to the leaves and spreads the leaves out in the sunlight. As plants grow larger, stems have to grow thicker to support the weight. Woody plants that grow higher than ten feet are usually called trees. Woody plants shorter than ten feet are called shrubs.

Within the roots and trunks of trees are two sets of "tubes" which transport food and water throughout the plant. **Xylem** cells carry the water from the roots to the leaves. As a plant grows, new xylem cells are made outside the old ones. The old xylem forms a woody center to the stem, which strengthens it. A plant that lives for several years has a woody center that grows thicker every year. **Phloem** cells carry food from the leaves to the rest of the tree.

Water-storing trunks
Semidesert trees have wide trunks that can store water to last through droughts. The xylem cells can hold water like a sponge.

Special roots

Most plants cannot live in very wet soil because they cannot get enough oxygen. In some trees the roots grow upward into the air. These are called **aerial roots**. Anchoring a 100-foot tree takes a lot of strength, so many tropical trees have **buttress** or **stilt roots** to help support them.

Large numbers of trees growing close together also help to support each other. Some plants, called **epiphytes**, grow on the tropical trees and send down aerial roots to collect water. In dry areas, plant roots grow deep into the soil to find water or spread out just under the surface to collect the dew.

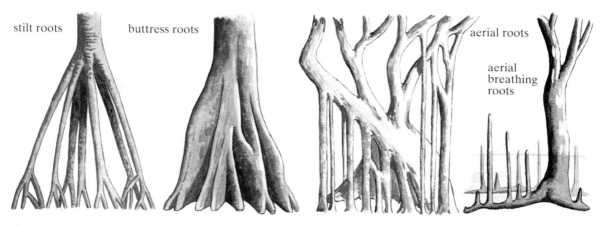

stilt roots   buttress roots   aerial roots   aerial breathing roots

Annual rings

In seasonal tropical forests and monsoon forests, there is a dry season. When water is scarce the tree does not grow as much as it does when there is plenty of water. This shows on the tree's stump. The cells formed in the dry season make a ring of small cells. The wet season cells

show as a ring of large cells. These rings together are called annual rings, because one of each grows every year. Tropical rain forests do not have a dry season and so growth continues all year round. There are no annual rings. That is why the trunks of rain forest trees make such hard timber.

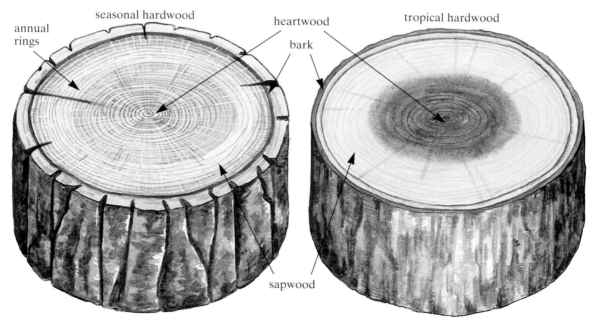

annual rings   seasonal hardwood   heartwood   bark   tropical hardwood   sapwood

A CANOPY OF LEAVES

The leaves are the "food factories" of the plant. The green pigment **chlorophyll**, which is contained in special cells in the leaves called chloroplasts, absorbs sunlight. In a process called **photosynthesis**, the light's energy is used to combine carbon dioxide from the air and water from the soil to make sugar. During this process the gas oxygen is produced and released into the air. The sugar is made into starches, fats, oils, or cellulose and carried to all parts of the tree by phloem cells.

Leaves use the water that comes up the trunk from the roots in the soil. The heat of the sun evaporates or changes the water into a gas, water vapor, which is lost through the leaves. More water moves up the trunk from the roots to replace the lost water. The movement of water is called **transpiration**.

Tropical forests
Tropical rain forests usually have four layers.

The highest layer or story, the canopy, is made from the leaves of the trees that grow to 100 feet or more.

The next story, the understory is made from the leaves of the trees that grow to 70 feet. The leaves are usually larger than those in the canopy, to make sure that they get enough light to make food.

The third layer, or story, is the shrub layer, and includes all the trees that do not grow more than 30 feet. The plants growing there can live in deep shade, and their leaves are the biggest in the forest.

The fourth layer is on the ground, and is called the herb layer.

Different-shaped leaves

The shapes of leaves are very different in the different parts of the tropics. Where there is plenty of water, leaves are large. In the semidesert and desert, leaves are reduced to spines or scales so that the plant does not lose too much water from them. The casuarinas have scale leaves.

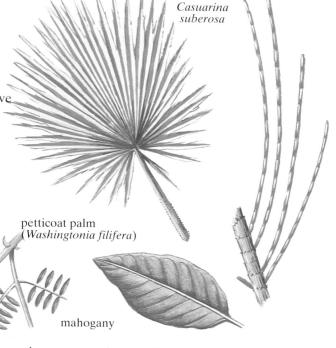

Casuarina suberosa

cycad

date palm

apiesdoring (*Acacia galpinii*)

petticoat palm (*Washingtonia filifera*)

mahogany

Drip tips and ponds

One leaf shape in particular, called the drip tip leaf, is found in the tropical rain forests. Drip tips are found on many different plants. They can be seen on the rubber plant (*Ficus elastica*), which comes from the Asian rain forests. The leaves curve down to the center rib, which runs down to a point. The leaf is shaped so that rain will drip off it, down to the ground and the root system. Cycads and some palms have leaves shaped to drain the water the other way, toward the base of the leaf and the stem.

Ficus leaves with drip tip

cycad "pond"

23

TROPICAL FLOWERS

Most tropical trees are flowering plants. Although the flowers come in all shapes, sizes, and colors, they all have the same job to do. Flowers produce the male sex cell protected in **pollen** grains and the female sex cell or **ovule** in the **ovary**. When pollen is transferred from the male part of the flower (the **stamen**) to the female part of the flower (the **carpel**), the male and female sex cells join to form a **seed** that will grow into the new tree. These seeds are often enclosed in a **fruit** (see p. 26). As plants cannot move about, they need wind or an animal to transfer pollen from one flower to another (**pollination**).

There is not much wind in a tropical forest and many different kinds of tree grow close together, so the chance of the pollen reaching another plant of the same kind is very small. Therefore most of the plants in tropical forests are pollinated by animals attracted to flowers by sight and by scent. Flowers produce a sweet substance called **nectar** that animals like to eat. If there is a nectar that they prefer, they will recognize the flower that produces it, and search for another like it. In doing so, they will carry pollen from one flower to another.

Figs and wasps

Flowers and animals evolved together in the old primary forests and now they depend on one another. For example, there are over 900 different figs (*Ficus* species) in the tropics, and each one is pollinated by a different wasp. The wasp lays its eggs in the flower and the grubs grow and feed there. The fig and the wasp depend on each other.

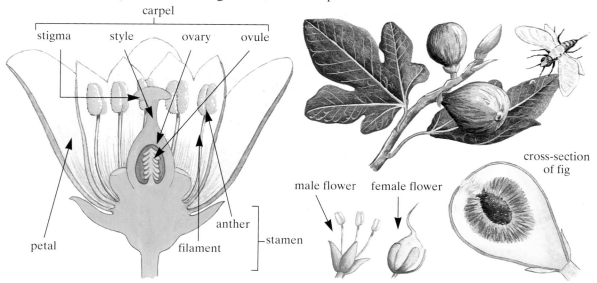

carpel

stigma style ovary ovule

petal

anther

filament

stamen

male flower female flower

cross-section of fig

Bats and Durian

Durian (*Durio zibethinus*) produce a large, thorny-looking fruit which is said to be one of the most delicious fruits in the world. Its drawback is that it smells terrible. It originated in Malaya, but it is cultivated all over Southeast Asia and is a valuable cash crop. The durian is pollinated by one kind of bat, which is attracted to the plant by the disgusting smell. This crop is in danger because the bats that pollinate its flowers are threatened. Many bats' roosts in caves were destroyed to get the limestone from them. The mangrove swamps, which grow other flowers that feed the bats when the durian is not in bloom, are being drained. With their food supply disappearing and their roosts being destroyed, the numbers of the bats are going down. Soon there will not be enough to pollinate the durian crops, and the farmers will lose their living. Now that the connection between bats and durian is known, their caves are no longer in danger. However, the swamps are still being drained and built on, so the fruit may soon be a rarity.

Bird pollinators

Birds like the tiny hummingbirds help to pollinate plants. Hummingbirds have long beaks and feed on nectar from trumpet-shaped flowers. The pineapple (*Ananas comosus*), a bromeliad, is also pollinated by hummingbirds.

FRUITS AND SEEDS

The job of fruit is to protect the seeds and attract animals that can carry the seeds away from the parent tree. The seeds of tropical fruits are usually large because they contain large amounts of food. The seeds begin growing on the floor of the tropical rain forest, where there is very little sunlight. They live on the stored food until they have grown leaves that are large enough to make the amount of food needed for a tree to grow.

Most of the seeds are contained in delicious, juicy fruits that the animals enjoy eating. The fruits are carried by them for long distances and the seeds fall to the ground a long way from the parent tree. The seeds have to be taken away, or dispersed, because if they fell to the ground under the parent tree, very few would survive. The parent tree is already using all the mineral salts from the soil under the tree, and its leaves are trapping most of the sunlight. The seeds must be taken to a patch of new ground to make sure that as many as possible **germinate** and grow into new trees.

Fruits of the forest
The seeds of tropical rain forest trees are spread by animals. Many seeds are enclosed in juicy fruits that are attractive to animals because they are a good food. Animals eat the fruits; the seeds are not broken down in the animal's gut, but pass out in their droppings. Other trees produce seeds that are themselves good to eat. In some cases seeds are dropped by the animals as they carry them to their nests.

Human distribution

People are the best distributors of fruits and seeds from tropical trees, as many tropical fruits are juicy and taste pleasant. People have taken many tropical fruit trees to new countries and continents to cultivate them as crops. Oranges, peaches (*Prunus persica*), bananas, and mangos all came from Asia. Pineapples and avocado pears originally came from tropical America, and dates from Africa.

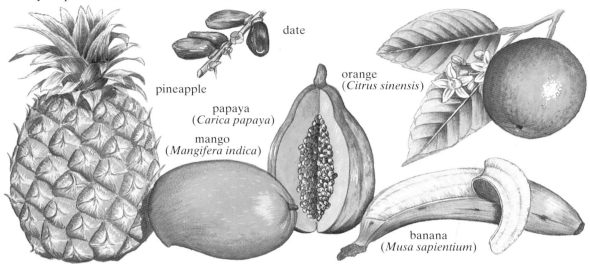

date

pineapple

papaya
(*Carica papaya*)

mango
(*Mangifera indica*)

orange
(*Citrus sinensis*)

banana
(*Musa sapientium*)

Food from nuts

Nuts are seeds but they were not meant to be eaten; their hard shells are designed to protect them. However, many animals, especially those that hoard food, collect nuts. Brazil nuts, walnuts, and cashew nuts (*Anacardium occidentale*) are spread by animals such as rats, porcupines, squirrels, and hamsters, as well as by people.

Cones and seeds

Gymnosperms like cycads, bunya pines, and monkey puzzle trees produce male and female cells in cones. The seeds are not enclosed in a fruit but lie naked within the female cone. Many birds and lizards feed on these seeds. Tapirs eat the seeds of Amazonian monkey puzzle trees (*Araucaria araucana*).

TROPICAL WETLANDS

Most trees cannot grow in water because the roots cannot get enough oxygen. However, there are some tropical trees that thrive on regular flooding.

The mangroves that protect the coasts of Africa and Asia grow on mudflats and along shores, where they are covered by saltwater twice a day. The tangle of their roots protects the soil, preventing it from washing away when the tide goes down.

In parts of the river systems with a heavy rainfall, where the land is very flat, the forests are often flooded for up to half the year. The parts of the Amazon basin called **varzeas**, and land around the Mekong River in Cambodia, are flood forests. The water in these forests is not always shallow – the varzeas may be flooded with 40 feet of water. Only the canopy, the top layer of the forest, remains above the flood water.

Mangrove swamps

There are several different species of tree growing in the mangrove swamps. The mangrove *Rhizophora* has stilt roots that support it in the wet, shifting mud. *Avicenna* has roots that grow upward, into the air, to take in oxygen from the air when the roots are covered in muddy water. The woven roots protect many small animals. Fishes and shellfish, particularly, multiply in mangrove swamps. The "walking" fishes called mudskippers climb out of the water and up the aerial roots and trunks of the mangroves.

Animals of the flood forests

Small land animals like rats climb the trees of the flood forests and live in the canopies until the waters go down again. Monkeys and two-toed sloths can still move about in the high branches, and birds and bats continue to feed above the water.

Floating food

The trees of flood forests are unusual as the seeds are often transported long distances by water instead of being spread by animals. These seeds provide food for the fishes that feed among the tree trunks. Fishes crack the hard cases of some nuts, which helps the nuts to germinate and grow when the waters go down.

These seed-eating fishes are hunted by large flesh-eating fishes, and by freshwater dolphins. One of the largest of the freshwater fishes, the pirarucu, which grows to 8 feet, lives in the Amazonian flood forests. Fishes grow very quickly in the flood forests, and in Cambodia people make use of this by having fisheries in parts of the flood forests.

TROPICAL GRASSLANDS

Not all tropical trees live in the moist forests. Some grow in the dry parts of the tropics, where there is not enough rain to allow large numbers of big plants to grow. Grasses and flowering plants cover the ground, and there are a few trees, spaced out where there is not much water, and growing as **scrub** where there is enough water.

Some of the trees of the grasslands have very long roots which grow down to reach water supplies deep underground. Others have very shallow roots, spread out over a large area, so that they can collect the dew. Some trees store water in their trunks to last through the dry periods. The leaves are small, and may have a waterproof surface that stops too much evaporation of water from the leaves.

The trees also need protection from hungry animals. Many of them have long spines, like the *Acacias* – the African thorn trees. Others, like some *Euphorbias*, have unpleasant-tasting sap that stops animals from eating them. Many of these trees of the dry tropics are now used to help trees to grow again in places where the forests have been cut down and the soil has washed away. As they are adapted to dry conditions, they can grow where the forest trees cannot. Once they have stopped soil erosion, the forest trees can be planted again, and in time the forest will return.

Trees that store water

Storing water is one way trees make sure they can live through long dry seasons. African and Australian baobabs use this method to survive (see p. 11). The roots spread out over a large area, collecting dew and rain when it falls. The trees store the water in the soft tissues in the trunk, and a tree that is 70 feet high may be 60 feet around its trunk.

In Australia, the barrel tree (*Brachychiton rupestre*) solves its water problems in the same way. The trunk of the tree is swollen to store water for use during the dry season.

tree at end of wet season

tree at end of dry season

The useful eucalyptus

Eucalyptus trees originally came from Australia. They are the gum trees that grow so well in dry places. They have been useful to people in the past because the oil in eucalyptus leaves helps to clear blocked noses and sinuses. Today they are playing an important part in conservation. Eucalyptus trees grow very fast, even in fairly dry conditions, and they are now grown to provide firewood in Africa and Asia.

The thorn trees

Thorn trees are the trees on which many of the African animals feed, even though they have long spines. Giraffes, antelopes, and domestic animals manage to feed on the leaves and seed pods. Thorn trees, like gum trees, are now being planted in areas with soil erosion. They help to bind the soil and allow the original trees to grow again.

ANIMALS OF THE FORESTS

Scientists think that there are at least 90,000 different plants in the tropical forests, which is more than one-third of all the plants on the planet. Tropical forests also provide a home for many different animals.

Most of the mammals that live in the forests are adapted to living in the trees. Besides gorillas, gibbons, chimpanzees, and orangutans, there are large numbers of bats and gliding mammals, such as the flying squirrel, flying phalanger, and flying dormouse. The Indian elephant, the tiger, and the rhinoceros are also forest mammals.

Birds are particularly suited to life in the forest branches, and there are 2,600 different kinds of tropical forest birds. Their sizes range from a bumblebee-sized hummingbird to the large monkey-eating harpy eagles.

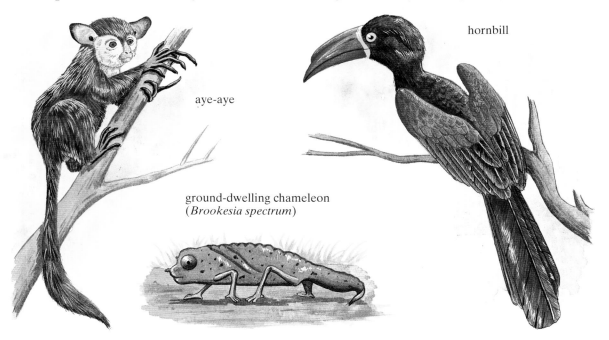

aye-aye

hornbill

ground-dwelling chameleon
(*Brookesia spectrum*)

Africa and Madagascar

The continent of Africa, including Madagascar, has many unusual animals. Aye-ayes are so strange that they are a family all to themselves. Coming out at night, they feed on fruit and the insect grubs in the tree branches. Their forest home is in danger from clearing and so they are an endangered species.

Slow-moving chameleons have eyes that can move in different directions and four long toes that allow them to grip twigs. They shoot out their long, sticky tongues to catch insects to eat.

Hornbills of African and Asian tropical forests pick fruit and catch insects with their great beaks. The beaks are light, with spongy bone in them.

Many frogs, lizards and snakes live in the trees, with "flying" examples of each. In the streams, ponds, and rivers there are many fishes – about 3,000 in Amazonia alone. Add to these the millions of insects, spiders, millipedes, and centipedes, and it is easy to see that one-third of the animals in the world could live in the tropical forests.

python

bowerbird

pheasant

gibbon

Asia and Australia

The green tree python lives in the forests of New Guinea. Its green color and coiled loops camouflage it among the leaves. It is very similar to the emerald tree boa, from South America. The bowerbirds, a unique Australian group, live on the forest floor.

Pheasants live in the Asian forests. The beautiful Argus pheasant is found in swampy, lowland forest in Borneo, Sumatra, and Malaysia.

The lar gibbon lives in the tropical trees of Borneo and Malaysia, feeding on fruit, leaves, eggs, and birds. Its long arms allow it to swing through the treetops from branch to branch.

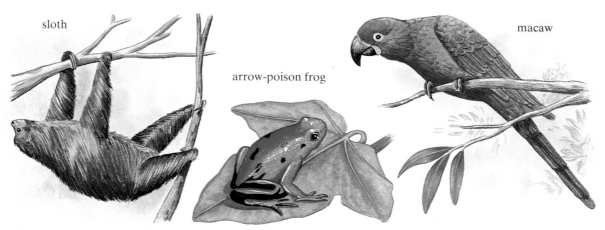

sloth

arrow-poison frog

macaw

South America

Central and South American tropical forests have a great number of animals living in them. Many arrow-poison frogs spend almost all their lives in the trees, although a few feed on the forest floor. The brilliantly colored macaws live in flocks, feeding on nuts. Sloths are completely adapted to living in trees, hanging from branches. Sloths themselves are a home for other plants and animals. One sloth had an alga, three different beetles, three kinds of moth, and six different mites living on it!

TREES, AIR, AND WARMTH

Tropical trees are linked with the air, or atmosphere, all around the Earth and also with the warmth of the planet. The reason is that trees do not reflect light, but trap the energy of the sun. They use some of this energy for photosynthesis and the rest warms the leaves and the surrounding air. Tropical forests absorb between 85 and 93 percent of the sunlight falling on them.

Areas with fewer plants do not absorb as much warmth and light. Deserts lose their heat at night because there are few plants to hold the warmth. The poles are very cold because they only absorb 10 to 15 percent of the sun's energy.

Tropical plants also help to keep the balance among the gases in the air. When plants make food they use carbon dioxide and water to make sugar and oxygen (see p. 22). Carbon dioxide is released into the air when animals and plants respire or breathe, and when plants, coal, and oil are burned. Plants reuse the carbon dioxide when it returns to the air.

Tropical forest "pump"
The large areas of tropical forest have warm air surrounding the trees. Warm air rises. The tropical forest's warm, moist air rises up into the atmosphere. More cool air moves into the forest to take its place and that is warmed in turn. The warm air in the atmosphere moves away from the equator toward the poles as winds. These currents warm the land and the sea as they move over them. Warm air passing over the sea picks up more moisture. These warm, wet winds change as they cool. Clouds form and rain falls. Moisture that began in the tropical rain forest can fall as rain thousands of miles away.

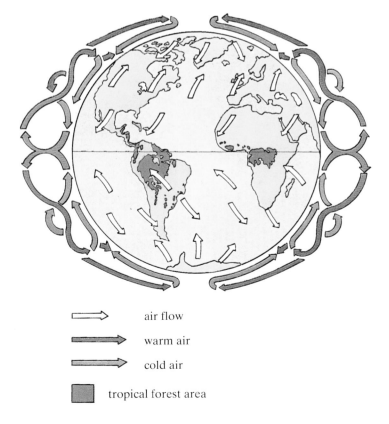

air flow

warm air

cold air

tropical forest area

The "Greenhouse" Effect

The tropical forests are very important in keeping the amount of carbon dioxide in the air at a constant level. Carbon dioxide is one of the so-called "greenhouse gases" that trap infrared radiation or heat rays from sunlight, thus warming up the atmosphere. Some warming is essential, for without the natural greenhouse effect the Earth would be much cooler and life as we know it could not exist. However, if too much carbon dioxide is produced and not enough removed, the atmosphere could warm up too much. This could cause enormous problems, such as melting of the icecaps. The tropical forests use up vast amounts of carbon dioxide, so if they are cut down the amount of this gas in the air will increase. Also, forests are being cleared by burning, which in itself produces vast amounts of carbon dioxide. Most of the other dangerous gases such as nitrous oxide, methane, ozone, and chlorofluorocarbonates (CFCs) come from human activities. People are now aware of the problems, and steps are being taken to cut down production of greenhouse gases.

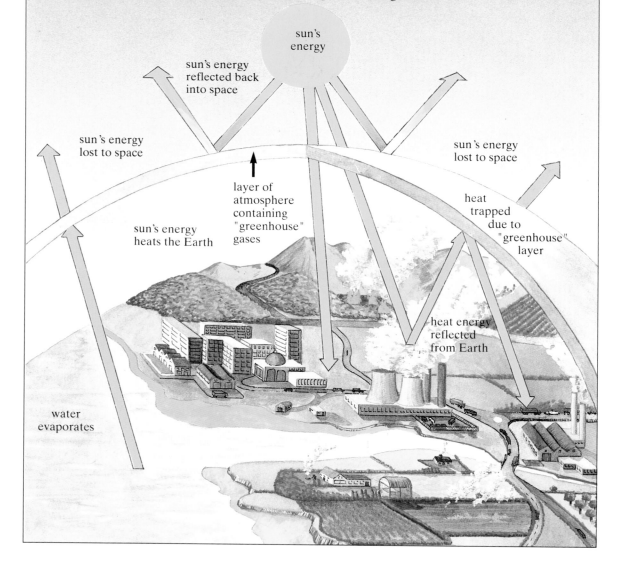

sun's energy

sun's energy reflected back into space

sun's energy lost to space

sun's energy lost to space

layer of atmosphere containing "greenhouse" gases

heat trapped due to "greenhouse" layer

sun's energy heats the Earth

heat energy reflected from Earth

water evaporates

TREES, RAIN, AND RIVERS

Tropical rain forests receive about half the rain that falls on the Earth. Some tropical rain forests have 300 inches of rain fall on them in one year. They act like a giant sponge, soaking up water. The raindrops trickle down the branches and trunks and drip from the leaves. The water reaches the soil as a fine spray, and gently soaks into it. The trees' roots take in the water and pass it back up the trunk to the leaves. As water dries from the leaves, some of it rises into the atmosphere where it forms clouds.

The forests also stop water from rushing downriver all at once. The trees slow down the water and some of it trickles down into the ground. The water takes a long time to reach the rivers and so helps to keep them flowing steadily throughout the year. The river will flood sometimes, when melting snows pour large amounts of water into streams and rivers. However, the forest prevents a flood after every rainstorm.

Protecting the soil

Tropical forests also protect the soil and the water supply. If the trees were not there, the soil would receive the full force of heavy raindrops. The fertile soil would quickly turn to mud and be swept away, exposing the hard, infertile soil below. Rivers, pools, and lakes would fill up with mud. The rivers would become shallower and more likely to flood. Where rain forests have been cut down the land has become barren and useless.

Tropical floods

People have only just begun to understand how the tropical forests protect the soil and the water supply. In the past, forests have been cut down and trees sold as timber or burned for fuel. The land was left exposed to the torrential rain. The soil was washed away and the rivers flooded. This has happened many times in China, Bangladesh, India, Burma, and Sarawak.

Saving the forests

The governments of tropical countries are beginning to protect their forests. Tree poachers cutting illegal timber in Thailand can be prosecuted and shot. Governments are trying to stop the cutting of primary forests, and are giving money to forestry departments to replant lost forest. Unfortunately, there are still people who cut timber and smuggle it out of the country. It has been estimated that over 1.3 billion cubic yards of wood was illegally exported from the Philippines in 1981.

Many tropical trees are cut down to make paper or to be used as firewood. Many countries now plant fast-growing trees for burning. *Calliandra calothyrus*, from Central America, is now being planted throughout the tropics as firewood. It grows to 13 feet in a year and can then be cut down to 20 inches, when it will sprout many side branches.

FOOD OR FORESTS?

The tropical trees of the world are in danger today, and mostly from people. There are a great many people on the planet and they all want food and a place to live. Even today, the number of people is getting larger, and they will need even more space in the future.

The population in the tropical countries is growing faster than in most other countries. The people living there need land on which to grow food and houses to live in. So they have cut down many tropical trees to grow crops and for the timber.

There have always been farmers in the tropical forests, but in the past they were small groups of forest people. They would cut down the trees to make a clearing, burn off the plants to clear the ground, and plant their crops. When the poor soil no longer gave them good crops, they moved on to make a new clearing. They were called "slash-and-burn" farmers. The small groups would work in a circle, moving on every few years until, after 10 to 25 years, they would return to an old clearing. They did not damage the forests.

The new farmers
The new slash-and-burn farmers do not fully understand the ecosystem of the forests. They begin clearing at the edges of the forests and move inward. Behind them come the commercial farmers, planting sugarcane or tropical crops like cassava to sell. The forest is not given a chance to grow again, and the trees that once grew on that land are lost forever.

Disappearing forests

Each new farmer does not take a lot of land, but there are so many of them that the forests are being eaten away. In the poorer countries of the world there are 800 million people without land who are trying to farm. Many of them live in the tropics, and have to use forest land to live.

The forests of Thailand covered 53 percent of the country in 1960. By 1980 they only covered 23 percent. The Philippine Islands were 55 percent tropical forest in 1950, but by 1980 the forests only covered 35 percent. Between 1960 and 1980 the world lost 800,000 square miles of tropical forests.

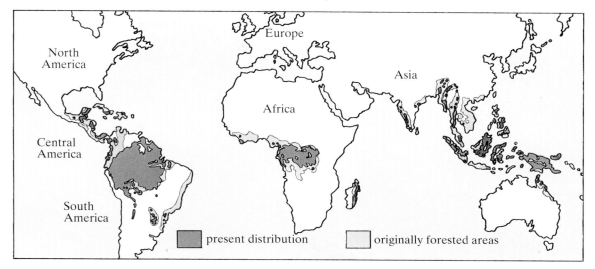

Trees and cattle

People do not only want vegetables to eat. The richer parts of the world eat a lot of meat. The poorer parts of the world are cutting down their tropical forests to make pasture for cattle. They export the beef so that the country can earn some money. The richer countries buy the beef because it is cheaper than their own beef.

Central America is losing its forests at the rate of about 8,000 square miles a year. The lean, grass-fed cattle are exported for much-needed money. In 1960, the forests covered 97,300 square miles of Central America. By 1980, 25,100 square miles had disappeared and pasture land for cattle had increased by 8,500 square miles.

39

TROPICAL TREASURE-TROVE

One problem with tropical forests is that they have not been fully explored. There is still a great deal about them that is not known. Scientists have found about 90,000 plants in the forests, but they think that there are at least another 30,000 waiting to be discovered, named, and studied. There could be a treasure-trove of useful plants to add to the many tropical plants that already help people. The scientists need time to find them. Time is running out because the forests are being destroyed so fast. Plants are becoming extinct (dying out) as people cut and burn down the forests to make room for more food, for homes, or to use the timber.

The world could be losing a cure for cancer and many other diseases, a supply of oil, a food that could feed the starving, or wild relatives of domestic plants that are resistant to diseases. If scientists are not given time to look at the plants and animals of tropical forests, we will never know what we have lost.

Tropical forest pesticides

Human-made pesticides can damage ecosystems, but there are natural pesticides which decay like any other plant when they have done their work. Pesticides such as rotenoids are made from the roots of plants that grow in the forests of Southeast Asia and the Amazon. Over 60 different kinds of plants are used, including a woody liana, derris (*Derris* species). Their powdered roots get rid of pests but do not harm birds and mammals. Tropical trees in Papua New Guinea, such as *Toona* species, also produce chemicals that keep ants away from them. There may be plant pesticides to replace all the chemical pesticides, but they have to be found first. Tropical forests are a good place to start looking.

Tropical sweeteners

Today, when people are worried about eating too much sugar, there might be a use for the sweeteners found in the tropical forests. West African forests alone can produce two. The berries of the tropical woody shrub miracle fruit (*Synsepalum dulcificum*) makes even lemons taste sweet. The serendipity shrub berry (*Dioscoreophyllum cumminsii*) is 3,000 times sweeter than sugar. Another West African fruit, the katemfe (*Thaumatococcus danielli*) produces a sweetener that is already in use.

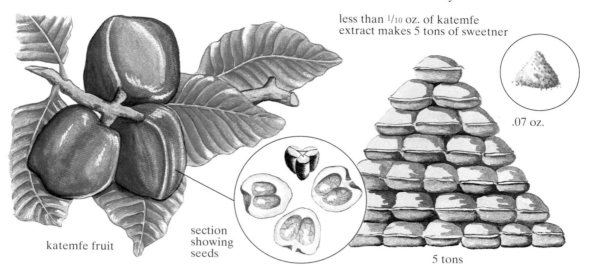

less than 1/10 oz. of katemfe extract makes 5 tons of sweetner

.07 oz.

katemfe fruit

section showing seeds

5 tons

Tropical forest oils

The fuels used by people today – coal, oil, and natural gas – are called fossil fuels. This is because they are the remains of plants that lived millions of years ago. Fossil fuel supplies will not last forever, and there is no way of replacing them. Scientists are looking at fast-growing tropical oil palms (*Elaeis guineensis*) to see if they can use the energy trapped in them. They are now cultivated on plantations for their oil. A similarly useful tree, the babassu palm (*Orbignya oleifera*) grows in the Amazon forest.

41

SAVING THE FORESTS

All over the world people are beginning to realize what is happening to their world and are beginning to do something about it. Until the 1950s, the tropical forests were virtually untouched. By 1975, 20 percent had been cut down and it is estimated that if destruction continues at the same rate over 50 percent of the forest will have disappeared by the year 2000.

The problems are so great that many international groups are working to save the forests. They do so by teaching governments and people the importance of the tropical trees in the world's **ecosystem**. The oldest group working for conservation, the Food and Agricultural Organization of United Nations (FAO), was formed in 1945, and teaches people new ways of farming that will not damage their land.

The International Union for the Conservation of Nature and Natural Resources (IUCN), formed in 1948, works with governments. It advises them of plants and animals that are in danger of extinction and the best way to save them. In 1961, IUCN formed the World Wildlife Fund, now called the World Wide Fund for Nature (WWF), which raises money to save endangered plants and animals.

Rubber-tapping

Some people have always taken care of their surroundings. The rubber tappers who take rubber, or latex, from the wild rubber trees in Brazil do so very carefully. They know that the trees need time to recover after they have been tapped. Each tapper has three trails through the forest, and they use them one after the other. The trees are tapped once every three days. They continue to grow and give rubber.

Korup National Park

In Cameroon, West Africa, the government has promised to protect 20 percent of its land. It has done so in time. There are still some parts of the tropical forests that are untouched. Korup National Park is a good example. It was declared a forest reserve in 1937 and became a fully protected national park in 1986. Apart from conserving the wildlife, Korup plans to provide the people living around it with meat, so that they will not be driven to poaching from the park. It will use tourism to educate people on the need to preserve the wildlife.

"Hug the trees"

In India the village women began their "hug the trees" or Chipko campaign. When men arrived to cut down trees around a village, each woman hugged a tree. In the past some women were hurt, or even killed. Today the "hug the trees" custom is protecting Indian forests. The women are starting to replant the forests, using the wild plants that they use every day. The ordinary people are helping to save their forests.

GLOSSARY

AERIAL ROOTS – Plant roots that grow up from the soil or water into the air, or which grow from a plant high off the ground into the soil.

ANGIOSPERMS – Plants with flowers and seeds that grow into fruit.

BIOME – A large, stable community of plants and animals. For example, deserts and rain forests are biomes, each with its own group of plants and animals.

BOTANIST – A scientist who studies plants and their lives.

BUTTRESS ROOTS – Plant roots that grow out to form supporting ridges around the base of a tree to help keep it upright.

CARPEL – The female part of a flower, made up of a stigma, a style, and an ovary.

CHLOROPHYLL – The green pigment in plants that traps the energy of the sun needed for photosynthesis.

CROWN – The top branches and leaves of a tree.

ECOSYSTEM – A community of plants and animals living together and depending on one another. An ecosystem may be small, like a pond, or large, like a biome.

EPIPHYTES – A plant that grows in the air supported by another plant.

FRUIT – The part of a flower that contains and protects the developing seed or seeds.

GERMINATE – The sprouting of a seed to give a new plant.

GYMNOSPERMS – Nonflowering trees that have seeds mostly contained in woody cones, or in fleshy scales.

HABITAT – The place where a plant or animal lives. There are many different habitats, such as a mountain habitat or a woodland habitat.

HARDWOOD – Timber from the angiosperm trees, which are usually deciduous. However, not all hardwoods are hard. Balsa, for example, is a soft hardwood. Softwood comes from gymnosperm trees such as conifers.

LEACH – To wash mineral salts down into the soil. In rain forests the rain can wash salts down out of reach of plants, leaving poor topsoil.

NECTAR – The sugary liquid produced by flower petals to attract insects.

OVARY – The part of the flower that contains the ovule.

OVULE – The female cell in a plant that, after being fertilized by a male cell, becomes a seed.

PHLOEM – The long cells that form tubes around the outside of a tree, just under the bark. They carry food from the leaves to the rest of the plant.

PHOTOSYNTHESIS – The process that takes place in the leaves, where, in sunlight, carbon dioxide gas and water are turned into sugars and oxygen.

POLLEN – The male cell that joins with or fertilizes an ovule to make a seed.

POLLINATION – The movement of pollen grains, by animals, wind, or water, from one plant to another.

SCRUB – The small trees and bushes that grow in dry places, such as thorn scrub in Africa and eucalyptus scrub in Australia.

SEED – A fully developed, fertilized ovule. It contains an embryo (young plant) and a food store, and can grow into a new plant.

SPECIES – Plants or animals that look like each other and that can mate to produce fertile offspring like themselves.

STAMEN – The male part of the flower.

STILT ROOTS – Roots that grow out from the trunk above the ground, like stilts, and help support the tree.

TRANSPIRATION – The flow of water from the roots of a plant, up the stem, into the leaves, and out into the air.

VARZEA – The part of the Amazon basin that is regularly flooded. Plants in the varzeas have adapted to living underwater for long periods.

XYLEM – The long, woody tubes that carry the water from the roots to the rest of the tree. The woody heart of the tree trunk is made from xylem cells.

TREES IN THIS BOOK

Afrormosia (*Pericopsis elata*)
Allspice (*Pimenta dioica*)
Amazonian monkey puzzle (*Araucaria araucana*)
Apiesdoring (*Acacia galpinii*)
Avicenna species
Avocado pear (*Persea americana*)
Babassu palm (*Orbignya oleifera*)
Balsa (*Ochroma lagopus*)
Banana (*Musa sapientium*)
Banyan (*Ficus bengalensis*)
Baobab (*Adansonia digitata*)
Barrel or bottle tree (*Brachychiton rupestre*)
Brazil nut tree (*Bertholletia excelsa*)
Bunya pine (*Araucaria bidwilli*)
Calliandra (*Calliandra calothyrus*)
Cardomom (*Elletaria cardomomum*)
Cashew (*Anacardium occidentale*)
Casuarina suberosa
Cinchona (*Cinchona ledgeriana*)
Cinnamon (*Cinnamomum zeylanicum*)
Clove (*Eugenia caryophyllata*)
Coca (*Erythroxylon coca*)
Cocoa tree (*Theobroma cacao*)
Coconut palm (*Cocos nucifera*)
Coffee tree (*Coffea arabica*)
Cycads (*Cycas media; Cycas revoluta*)
Date palm (*Phoenix dactylifera*)
Derris (*Derris* species)
Diptocarpus species
Doum palm (*Hyphaene theobaica*)
Durian (*Durio zibethinus*)
Ebony (*Diospyros mespiliformis*)
Euphorbia species
Fig (*Ficus* species)
Ginger (*Zingiber officinale*)
Grass tree (*Kingsia australis*)
Greenheart (*Nectandra roediei*)
Guava (*Pisidium guajava*)
Honeysuckle tree (*Banksia marginata*)
Ipilpil (*Leucana leucocephala*)
Katemfe (*Thaumatococcus danielli*)
Mahogany (*Swietenia mahogani*)
Mango (*Mangifera indica*)
Melegueta pepper (*Aframomum melegueta*)

Miracle fruit (*Synsepalum dulcificum*)
Moreton Bay chestnut (*Castanospernum australe*)
Nutmeg (*Myrica fragrans*)
Obeche (*Triplochiton scleroxylon*)
Oil palm (*Elaeis guineensis*)
Orange (*Citrus sinensis*)
Pacific walnut (*Dracontomelum* species)
Papaya (*Carica papaya*)
Peach (*Prunus persica*)
Pepper (*Piper nigrum*)
Petticoat palm (*Washingtonia filifera*)
Rhizophora species
Rosewoods (*Dalbergia* species)
Rubber plant (*Ficus elastica*)
Rubber tree (*Hevea braziliensis*)
Sago palm (*Metroxylon sago*)
Sapele (*Entandophragma cylindricum*)
Screw pine (*Pandanus odoratissimus*)
Serendipity berry (*Dioscoreophyllum cumminsii*)
She-oak (*Casuarina equisitifolia*)
Southern beech (*Nothofagus* species)
Southern oak (*Castanopsis* species)
Sydney blue gum tree (*Eucalyptus saligna*)
Teak (*Tectona grandis*)
Thorn or gum arabic tree (*Acacia senegal*)
Toona species

FURTHER READING
For children
Conserving Rain Forests by Martin Banks;
Steck-Vaughn, 1989.
For adults
Guide to Tropical and Semi-Tropical Flora by
Loraine E. Kuck and Richard C. Tongg; C.E.
Tuttle, no date.
*Tropical Trees: Found in the Caribbean, South
America, ·Central America, Mexico* by Dorothy
Hargreaves; Ross Hargreaves, 1965.
In the Rainforest by Catherine Caulfield; Alfred
A. Knopf, 1985.
The Primary Source by Norman Myers; Norton,
1985.

INDEX

13161

582.160   Cochrane, Jennifer.
COC
         Trees of the
         tropics.